# GRAB IT

## THE THING
### Included

S. E. McKenzie

# DEDICATION
To everyone who has been left out in the cold

TABLE OF CONTENTS

THIS BOOK IS A BOOK OF SPECULATIVE FICTION ....................iv
TABLE OF CONTENTS.................................................................v
GRAB IT ....................................................................................2
I................................................................................................2
Grabber knew when Elaine was down ........................................2
II ...............................................................................................9
Black bird with yellow beak .......................................................9
III ............................................................................................12
As the hard line even got harder ...............................................12
THE THING ............................................................................15
I...............................................................................................15
The Thing attracted the eye .....................................................15
II .............................................................................................19
Soon Adam and Eve .................................................................19
III ............................................................................................19
"Boss won't disclose his plan for us .........................................19
IV ............................................................................................20
What makes Boss......................................................................20
V .............................................................................................24
Son from years gone by ............................................................24

VI ......................................................................................25
The thing will sing ........................................................25
VII .....................................................................................26
The Lie grew..................................................................26
VIII ...................................................................................31
Gentle child...................................................................31
IX......................................................................................32
Wild Spirit .....................................................................32
X........................................................................................33
The young ......................................................................33
XI......................................................................................34
There was no limit ........................................................34
XII ....................................................................................35
And I saw mercy............................................................35
XIII ..................................................................................35
Toxic man .......................................................................35
XIV ...................................................................................36
Bias grew the way it knew...........................................36

# GRAB IT

# GRAB IT

## I

Grabber knew when Elaine was down
For rumors were spread all over town.
Grabber knew when to pounce.

Elaine could not run
Nor bounce
Back into the life

That Grabber turned upside down.

Grabber
Spoke softly so Elaine could not hear
The fear of souls gone by.

The ones no one heard
When they cried out in pain
No one came

For there was no love in sight
Very few could free themselves
From their fright.

# GRAB IT: The Thing Included

Grabber knew military prestige
While Elaine was too naïve.
To learn fast.

That Grabber's smile would never last.

Fear so cold
Froze many in time
Until they grew old.

Grabber was wearing a smile
When he said that he would
Be around for a while,

Even after those others were gone.

Some mourned those missing last words
Now blunted swords of the mighty
For No one knew where they had gone.

And Elaine had no reason
To feel intimidated
While she was being initiated.

Grabber was overjoyed
When she said that she was not paranoid
Grabber was so elite no one could call him schizoid.

S.E. McKENZIE


Before he popped a steroid
And then shook his index finger
He faked not being annoyed

And he let this persona linger.

For Elaine was young and able
To work for free
For this was the new economy

The Cashless Society
Polarized in a mean way
Two sides fit together one way

And the grabber knew who to accuse
And he knew who to abuse
And he knew who to use.

Before he pulled out his gun
Some knew when to run
And leave all behind

For the land one day
Would grow back into nature;
And that hole in the wall

# GRAB IT: The Thing Included

Would become a perfect nest
For a beautiful bird
Some would call a pest.

The Grabber never knew what was best
And saw the savage
In what was wild

The Grabber grew old
Day by day
While he put tons of cash away.

Grabber would splash cash before the smash
And how he loved to consume
Tons of energy from people he never knew.

And that energy might renew
Into something new
And that was the best that Grabber could do.

And no one could ever be
Another Elaine
Or really ever understand her pain.

And how Grabber tried
To make a clone
Out of you too

S.E. McKENZIE

Before he grabbed land to pave
Over her grave there was a fence.
He said that a fence was his best defense.

What grew behind it was fodder for comics
Tragedy called new world order
So good for global economics

And power was nurtured so it could grow
Into a machine of sorrow
Within their dread, many faced tomorrow

When bad, the other side of good was turned around.

And in the end
Elaine's only friend
Was that bird living in a hole in a wall.

As you opened your door
He would sing to you and her every day;
A hello that brought cheer and was true

To yourself you must be
For all these things from days gone by
Will turn to rust and fade away; one day;

# GRAB IT: The Thing Included

As the grabber grew an invisible hand

"Money gave too much power to the underclass,"
Said the plutocrat
"Money would make them feel too much like an aristocrat

And imagine not knowing that
Or how to be a tool for a fool
That is why old school needs to be more cruel."

And Grabber said
"If you want to eat
Feel defeat

And kneel at my feet."
And Grabber knew Money grew in value
As demand grew out of hand.

Money gave freedom
And independence
From the plutocrat's command

For a few hours a day
Freedom from feudalistic
Never mystic; Society.

"And who is your Lord?"
Grabber asked.
"It is me, Lord of the land.

Sometimes called the invisible hand?
As Money was piling up inside Grabber's drawer
He took yours too before he left slamming your door.

He was so annoyed
Cause you were self-employed
And he wanted to return to cashless slavery

When he felt so much bravery.

In this new Economy
The age of the Cashless Society
Where everything was only free

Until you wanted more.

Grabber knew how to manipulate
Twist words around and control fate
And he knew how the oppressed loved to hate.

He never had to order the mass to behave
For the frame; all around their mind;
Shaped them to grow unkind.

# GRAB IT: The Thing Included

In the old world, in a land so far away
There was a mass grave that Grabber hid under
Another man's blunder

The anger was heard from afar
And thunder's rumble was the sound
As lightning's spark hit the ground

To make this land more fertile

## II
Black bird with yellow beak
What would you say if you could speak?
You carried a twig

For your nest
But the tree was now gone
Your nest was not seen

Your eggs were crushed
It was unforeseen
No one did it to be mean.

The negative bias
Let Grabber hide
Behind his Alias

But the black bird with the yellow beak
Was not fooled
He dropped his twig

And sang a tune
It was so sad
It brought a tear to my eye

Grabber did not care
For he had already chopped his wood
That is why the bird's tree was no longer there

And many said that the flood began
For Grabber never gave thanks
Even when the flood raged above its banks.

And it rained day after day
And there was too much rain
To soak into the ground

Where Elaine's friends were hidden
For it was forbidden
To hear ghosts speak

# GRAB IT: The Thing Included

And as the waters rose
The dam burst and came tumbling down
For the dam was above capacity

The flood was called another unforeseen tragedy
While this water so pure
Grew the wild forest that we all knew

As the water fed these living streams
The people were drowning
Amidst the sound of screams

Elaine could not feel their pain
While Grabber turned away
He had nothing to say

Though his greed
Freed
The deadliest force

The world had ever seen.

### III

As the hard line even got harder
Black bird with yellow beak
Looked all around but couldn't speak

Grabber didn't care about consent
All he wanted was his rent
And he didn't have much time to grow his content

And black bird with yellow beak
Flew in the sky so free
Then stopped to rest in a weed

That one day would grow into another tree.

And house black bird and his family
While Grabber had no time to feel empty
For there was so much for him to gain

As long as he closed his eyes
To all our pain.
As the barriers he built were beautified

# GRAB IT: The Thing Included

We all knew that Grabber had lied
And if we weren't so petrified
We would have tried

To hear the voices that could not be heard;
So far away and underground;
They were out of the way;

Their faint echo can still be heard today.

## THE END

S.E. McKENZIE

# THE THING

## THE THING

### I

The Thing attracted the eye
For it was in  plain sight,
Like a Temptress

It was forbidden.
The boss said so
And the cost would be Paradise lost.

To Eve's dismay
Adam ate the fruit anyway.
Some say the fruit's beauty

Led Adam astray.
Adam said he would not have
Lived life any other way.

"Feeling such pull
Had to be right."
Adam said,

Adam asked Eve,
"Have you ever felt anything
So tempting and alluring?"

"Yes, for love is even more enduring."

We must be aware of that Thing's pull
For it has the power to fool
And Boss told us to never break the rule

"Silence woman."
"Adam, we must take care
For Boss may force us to go."

"Eve,
I can't believe
That my love for this fruit is wrong

Look at me
This fruit
Has made me so strong."

"Adam don't you see
I need a gentle touch
Not a heavy hand

Show me the power of your love
And I will follow you
Across the land.

# GRAB IT: The Thing Included

I will stay true, I promise
Just stay by my side
Until life do us part,

Give me a gentle kiss
And I will be yours
In heavenly bliss.

Please don't go breaking my heart."

"Eve, I am stuck in a rut
Living with you in this hut
I wanna get out"

"Adam I am begging you please
I am down on my knees
Please do what is right

And I will follow
Where you lead
And all I need

Is that gentle love
I used to know.
Adam where did it go?"

"Eve do not grieve;
When I taste forbidden fruit
I am a stronger man

My faith is renewed in who I am;
And nothing steps in my way
Cause I am that kind of man.

So woman don't feed your fear
And give me space to breathe
I am who I am

And to that thought I hold dear."

"Adam, it is your greed that feeds my fear."
"Eve, I must be the strongest man that I can be."
"Adam show me that gentle touch

That I love so much
I don't need a heavy hand
For it turns my love sour;

Put down that forbidden fruit
And go pick a flower
That I can put in my hair."

# GRAB IT: The Thing Included

I need that old time love
That I used to know,
Adam where did it go?

## II

Soon Adam and Eve
Felt the state of undress.
Boss blamed the fruity Temptress

"Adam I was not kidding
I think we were too willing
To eat forbidden fruit

It was all wrong
Its pull was way too strong
It was probably stringing us along."

## III

"Boss won't disclose his plan for us
For He is King of land and sky;
Adam must obey just to get by."

**IV**
What makes Boss
Think he is so elite?
Why should I say I was wrong

When forbidden fruit made me so strong?

Why should I agree to my defeat?
I am a man
I will eat what I want to eat.

I will not let such fruit rot
Nor let our opportunity
For empowerment be shot."

"Adam, I felt the pull too
Tree of Life felt so supernatural
And with new knowledge from that Tree

We now know Diversity

A chance to grow empathy;
For lovers with a heavy hand
Are never in demand.

# GRAB IT: The Thing Included

"Eve, did you feel that tingling sensation too?
Whenever that fruit is near
I mean near enough to touch

I can't say no
I love that fruit
So much."

"Yes I did
And its power over you makes me fear.
Why did it have to be in sight and be so near?

Why did it give you so much might?
There is something about that Thing
Which was never right."

"Eve, what shall we call that Thing?"

"Boss calls it Temptation
Must be a tool to tempt a fool;
A trick of a master who is very cruel;

It was forbidden now boss will make a scene,
He could get mean,
Even scream,

S.E. McKENZIE

For he is the king of the land and sky."

"Eve hold your tongue
And think of our young
Who have the right to this might."

"Adam, we shall teach our young grace
And to know their place
So they never question the boss

For his the king of land and sky.

If we prevent our young
From growing too mighty
We won't have to watch them die.

Clearly eating such fruit will be our loss
We were better off
When we obeyed the boss."

"Eve, It would have been
Another opportunity wasted
Just another fruit never tasted."

# GRAB IT: The Thing Included

"Adam you know what we were told."
Adam interjected.
"I am a man and yearn to be free.

Eve listened
With disdain and dread
And then replied
I must see the world which surrounds me

I must taste its fruit whenever I can
So I can feel like a free man.
I know we should be satisfied

For we live in Paradise
How was I to know
The snake had lied?

Here good and evil do not divide
Snake said If we eat from that tree
Our Life may not end in Death."

We could gain eternal breath
And expand
Free from Boss' invisible hand."

S.E. McKENZIE

"Adam, don't be a fool
Life is so precious
Because it ends too soon.

We did not need to understand
Because we were living Life
Under Boss' invisible hand."

"Such life is not for me
For I yearn to be free
And to see the world around me.

Now life is a rut
Living with you
In this hut.

I want to see the sea
And climb the ladder
To Eternity.

**V**

Son from years gone by
Climbed the mountain
Cause he couldn't fly

He found himself all alone

# GRAB IT: The Thing Included

On that mountain made of stone
They said that one must atone
For generations gone by

And the son wondered why.

## VI

The thing will sing
Praise onto the thing
Even though one day

The thing will fade away.
And all we will have left
Is life and time

Then that too
Will one day
Fade away.

How can we see
Truth and Beauty
Through all this Fog and War?

It is all around us
If we able to see
Life's living fragility.

Or if we do not see
It may be all blown away
By all this rush to fight

As death calls.

**VII**
The Lie grew
Between him
And you know who.

The Beast of hate
Shaped Fate.
The two edged sword

Was the tool
So cruel;
Gave power

To a fool
Who thought
It was his right to rule.

Hate grew
Between him
And you know who

# GRAB IT: The Thing Included

While Slander
Soothed his anger
For a moment or two.

The Beast sought power
Over the land;
He wanted absolute command.

As Hate grew
Hate began to cast a spell
Created the difference

Between Heaven and Hell.

And the beast wanted to rule
Everything in sight
For such power grew his might.

It didn't matter what was
Wrong or Right,
As long as he could win the Fight.

There was blood and gore
And he wanted more and more
For the Beast could not be satisfied;

So many died
And so many cried;
Some knew the Beast had lied.

This was the Age of Rage
While only Slander
Could soothe his anger

For a moment or two
Until he even tried
To target you.

He built
The Thing;
A new one every day

And he killed
Anyone
Who got in the way.

The power
Was organic and cosmic
Felt glorious and orgasmic

# GRAB IT: The Thing Included

He praised the thing;
He sung to the thing;
He became one with the thing.

And he wanted more.
The Beast grew;
As his hate was consumed

In this land where love once bloomed.
The Beast didn't care
Who was doomed;

His word was not designed
To better humanity
For his word

Was the tool of Slander

Soothed his anger
For a moment or two.
And the Beast said

"Take power
Any way you can,
For that is how

You will feel like a man."
And the Beast could not care
For he was just a fool.

He craved glory
And made up the rule
Behind walls to divide and conquer

The Saboteur used Slander
For it soothed his anger
For a minute or two.

And the son asked
"What should I do?"
And the old man replied

You must reach higher
Than the fighter
Dodge his negativity anyway you can

Only when you win
You will be treated
Like a man.

# GRAB IT: The Thing Included

Show the world some positivity
Then your light
Will shine

Upon the path you must follow

So do not avenge me
Make me proud
And go beyond

The narrow minded vision.
Don't be a tool for a fool
Make a better decision.

## VIII
Gentle child
Knew the path
For he took it every day

Until a monster-truck
Had parked in the way
Giving gentle child no right of way.

## IX

Wild Spirit
Vital and principal force
In all living matter

When broken
One is sadder
Some say badder

Walk away
To avoid being a target
A direct hit

As Toxic Man roams
He leaves widows
And burns homes

So many had fallen
Never knowing his name,
There was no one to blame?

No one at all.
It is up to you
To not fall

# GRAB IT: The Thing Included

During this urban war
No one cares
Who you are.

Toxic man
Talks, doesn't he love to talk
About equalization

But all there was
Was separation
A hurt sensation

For the last generation.

**X**
The young
Searched for truth
The innocence of youth

Was no more; they realized
The one they loved
Had lied.

And how they cried
When the promise was broken;
They ran into the crowd.

Bullets were flying all around
Many were shot
And had fallen down.

As the young were dying on the ground
The Wild Spirit
Flew in the wind.

And the Wild Spirit
Knew what had been done.
And the pain it grew

## XI

There was no limit
To the power
The Wild Spirit knew

Even though
Toxic Man owned
Almost everything in sight

Toxic Man was no match
For Wild Spirit's
Might

# GRAB IT: The Thing Included

So there was no freedom to be had.
Some felt sad
Many went bad.

Toxic man
Showed his bias proudly
His pride was shared loudly.

Toxic man;
Just another sad man
Who steps in the way
.

## XII
And I saw mercy
Crying through all our fear
For mercy tried to give

But Toxic Man
Would not allow
Mercy to live.

## XIII
Toxic man
Lives beneath
Wild Spirit

35

And above the fallen
Youth
Had been stolen

Now
Sad ghosts
Surround this ground

## XIV

Bias grew the way it knew
So Toxic Man was pulled too
And became trapped in his frame of mind

After he built this city
So pretty on a hill
Night time lights lit up

Promising a thrill
In his hand-me down town;
Time past it by.

Victorian age was left
For it made so many cry
Others fought to live

# GRAB IT: The Thing Included

Until it was their time to die.
Like the fruit on the tree
Fermented and pretty

Time wilted most things its true
Even me and you
Found glory in our love so true.

A time to live and a time to die
In this hand-me down city
Where most just drive by.

Souls were fenced in but not yet lost
They were just victims
Of a hidden opportunity cost.

Toxic man was surrounded
By the fake and snooty
He forgot about true love's beauty

That glowed in the night
Felt so right
Shone so bright.

Toxic man never questioned his loss;
So grateful was he
To be the boss.

Forgotten garden
From a long time ago
Was still home to ancient snakes

Who understood
Toxic man's mistakes.
The snakes could see the growing plumes,

They could smell the poisonous fumes.

Toxic man never knew
What he was fighting for
Until his fight was lost.

He returned to Wild Spirit that Day
And was granted new life as a bird
And then he flew away.

Never to be
An angel with wings
For he had been fooled by deadly things.

**THE END**

Produced by S.E. McKenzie Productions
First Print Edition April 2015

Enquiries: 1(778)992-2453
Mailing Address:
*S. E. McKenzie Productions*
*168 B 5th St.*
*Courtenay, BC*
*V9N 1J4*

Email Address:
messidartha@aol.com

http://www.amazon.com/SarahMcKenzie/e/B00H9RWX48/ref=ntt
_dp_epwbk_0